Teide

Teide National Park

EVEREST

Text: Francisco Javier Macías Martín

Photographs: Oliviero Daidola, Paolo Tiengo and Justino Díez

Layout: Gerardo Rodera

Cover design: Alfredo Anievas

Translation: EURO:TEXT, Martin Gell

SECOND EDITION
© EDITORIAL EVEREST, S.A.
Carretera León-La Coruña, km 5 - LEÓN
ISBN: 84-241-3526-1
Legal deposit: LE. 679-1998
Printed in Spain

EDITORIAL EVERGRÁFICAS, S.L.
Carretera León-La Coruña, km 5
LEON (Spain)

Teide

Tenerife is the largest of the Canary Islands (2,057 km^2) and, like most of the others, it features a rugged relief that is marked, amongst other things, by a mountainous ridge stretching across the island from the northeast to the southwest. The crowning glory of Tenerife, the Peak of El Teide, rises up from inside the Las Cañadas volcanic caldera, that great circular geological depression that forms the roof of the island. An impressive volcanic cone, El Teide soars to a height of 3,717 metres above sea level, which makes it the highest mountain in Spain.

Declared a National Park on 22nd January 1954, Las Cañadas del Teide has a surface area of 135 km^2 that extends into the districts of La Orotava, Guía de Isora, Santiago de Teide and Icod de los Vinos. The geological origin of the area has been the subject of much debate amongst scientists. According to Carracedo, El Teide and Las Cañadas are the result of an episode of volcanic activity that occurred about three million years ago and which led to the creation of a great dome standing between 3,000 and 5,000 metres high. On the other hand, Martínez de Pisón and Quirantes think more along the lines of the formation of an irregular geological structure dotted with valleys. Araña believes the process involved several phases and an equal number of eruptions. Nowadays, the prevailing theory is that of the great dome, albeit in slightly varying interpretations. Discrepancies still exist regarding the origin of the Las Cañadas depression, that enormous caldera encircling the peak and marked by a great wall measuring 12 by 17 km. The most favoured hypothesis is that contemplating the collapse of the volcanic dome. Inside Las Cañadas, to the north of this 'natural amphitheatre', we come across the geological ensemble of El Teide-Pico Viejo which, similar in appearance to a truncated cone, rises some 1,700 metres from its base. In reality, what we have before us here is a mountain formed by the eruption and subsequent superposition of several volcanoes: Pico Viejo, Montaña Blanca, Pico Cabras and Narices del Teide.

Visiting the National Park.

Preceding two-page spread: El Teide as seen from Los Roques.

The "Sea of Clouds" drifting over the Park.

Two-page spread overleaf: the snow-capped El Teide.

Crowning the structure is the Pan de Azúcar or Pilón which, rising up from the depression called La Rambleta, still features fumaroles or steam vents, an unmistakable sign that the volcano remains active. Over the last few centuries there has been a succession of eruptions, the most important of which being that which came about in the late 18th century, giving shape to what we know today as Pico Viejo. The last time El Teide exploded was earlier this century, the eruption taking place at Narices del Teide on the western slope of the cone. For many the true symbol of the Canary Islands, El Teide can be seen from most parts of the archipelago. This is especially the case in winter, when its snow-capped peak is a common sight, the snow occasionally extending down the mountainsides to cover the adjacent sections of Las Cañadas. At the foot of the mountain lies the Llano de Ucanca, an extensive plain bordered by the Roques de García to the north, by the limits of lava flows to the west and south, and by the wall of the Ucanca Summit to the east.

All over Las Cañadas, numerous solidified lava flows are to be found. Indeed, this is an area characterized by

On these pages
we can see...

...the geological variety
of the Park.

12

the so-called *malpaís* ('bad land') landscape, in which we can discover multi-coloured lava layers, in particular at Los Azulejos in the vicinity of the Parador Nacional. Also to be seen next to these lava formations are volcanic bombs (globular lava masses) - some of which are very large -, *lapilli* (tiny volcanic fragments), and ash. Such then are the features of an environment whose boundaries are perfectly marked out to the south, east and west by high cliffs pierced by a series of valley-floors and *cañadas* or ravines that are known, logically enough, as Las Cañadas del Teide. Gradually, materials transported in the process of erosion have come to fill in these original channels, thus giving rise to more or less extensive plateaux.

The *cañadas* were known to man way

13

back in ancient times, when they were used by the native people of Tenerife, the Guanches, as routes for the transhumance or periodical transfer of their herds of animals. Indeed, the original inhabitants of Tenerife basically subsisted on livestock farming, so much so that the care of goats played a major role in the day-to-day existence of the various *menceyatos* or kingdoms into which the island was divided. Each of these political units governed over its own territory, although no such exclusive rights applied either to the mountain peaks or, oddly enough, to the areas of high mountains, including the Las Cañadas area itself, which was considered to be strips of common pastureland to which all farmers could take their herds in summer. This use of

Las Cañadas has been confirmed by the discovery of numerous archaeological remains. Furthermore, experts researching into the religion of the first settlers of the Canary Islands have revealed the meaning that the island mountains held for them.

Basically, they embodied a Manichaean or dualistic conception of the universe featuring one deity of good and another of evil, who in the case of Tenerife was called "Guayota" and was believed to reside inside "Echeide", that is, El Teide.

The snowy landscape of Las Cañadas.

14

The climate of the National Park shares the characteristics of that of high mountains, being conditioned, among other factors, by its altitude. Although it has an average temperature of around 9º C, temperatures are seen to vary widely from day-time to night. The insolation level is high and there is abundant precipitation, although the latter varies in the course of the year. Winter features heavy rainfall combined with snow, which falls above all on the northern slopes of El Teide and can last for several months. This is

not the case in Las Cañadas, however, where snow is present for a much shorter time. The harsh environmental conditions prevailing in the Park, the fluctuations in temperature and the factors of insolation and aridity, would lead us to believe that this were a landscape in which all interest lay in its geological make-up. Nothing could be farther removed from the truth. Amidst the remains of past volcanic episodes life is seen to prosper, a fact which is clearly demonstrated, above all in the spring months, by the extraordinary wealth of flora on display.

The plantlife here is overwhelmingly Macaronesian in origin, although a number of species are in fact endemic to the area, some being so rare that it should come as no surprise that they caught the eye of botanical experts as early as the 18th century. The most noteworthy of these plants are the El Teide broom (Spartocytisus supranubius) and the laburnum (Adenocarpus viscosus), which, often appearing in perfect union, simply dominate the surroundings. The tangled stems of the broom are to be seen all around; somewhat lethargic in the harsh winter months, it flourishes magnificently in May. Rivalling the scent and colour of the broom is the yellow-flowered stunted laburnum. We should also draw the reader's attention to such plant species as the graceful, yellow-flowered *hierba pajonera* (Descourainia bourgeana); the pinkish *alhelí del Teide* (Erysimum scoparium), to be found amidst the lava flows; the unsophisticated Teide daisy, which no-one would ever suspect to be endemic to the Park; the El Guanche rose and several varieties of cistus. Neither should we overlook the red viper's bugloss or *taginaste rojo* (Echium wildprettii), an impressive example of Macaronesian flora that revels on the steep mountain sides, featuring slender leaves and soaring reddish-hued flowers that do full justice to its name. Belonging to the same

Southern entrance to the Park. ▶

Climbing the peaks of the Park. ▶

El Teide, covered in snow.

family are the blue-flowered *taginaste azul* (Echium webbii) and the *taginaste picante* (Echium auberanium).

Way above, at a height of 3,000 metres and over, where the aforementioned species simply cannot survive, we find the emblematic variety of the Park, namely the Teide violet, considered by some to be the plant species that grows at the greatest altitude in Spain. Its outstanding feature is certainly not its size - at times it can scarcely be made out against the ground - but rather its scent and colour, which are truly unique during the time it is in bloom. Indeed, this is when the miracle of life is seen to pulsate all around, in sharp contrast to the aspect afforded by the park in winter, characterized by skeletal shrubs bereft of flowers and occasionally, when conditions turn out to be extreme, even adorned with icicles. There are very few tree species characteristic of this region to be found in the area enclosed by the Park. In

Two views of the Park.

The "Queen's Shoe". ▶

20

Los Roques.

fact, we can mention but two: the Canary cedar, a tree which, featuring a twisted trunk, is perfectly adapted to the harsh conditions of these heights, and the Canary pine, a limited number of which prosper on the sheer faces of the caldera walls.

Insects account for the greatest number and variety of fauna species to be found . in the Park, over four hundred having been identified. As is the case with plants, animal life here has also developed certain particular features, even though its diversity is not quite as notable. Besides the insects, one must not overlook the *lagarto tizón* (Lacerta galloti), a black lizard whose habitat extends as far as some fairly high ground. Mammals are represented here basically by certain varieties of bat, the most remarkable of which is the one known as the "mountain bat".

Different views of Llanos de Ucanca.

Two-page spread overleaf, Los Azulejos.

Completing the picture of animal life in the Park are its birds, amongst which we should mention the crow, the blue chaffinch, the great grey shrike, Koenig's partridge or *perdiz moruna* (Alectoris barbara koenigi), the kestrel, the beautiful hoopoe, as well as rock doves. Neither should we forget the presence of certain introduced species such as the mouflon, which together with the omnipresent rabbit constantly subjected to the necessary controls.

The Park can be reached by road from various points of the island. Taking Santa Cruz de Tenerife as a reference, one possible route starts from the capital of the island and climbs to La

The "Stone Rose" near the Park.   Mina de San José.

Northern lava formations.

Vegetation near the Park.

Preceding two-page spread: lava formations.

This page, Minas de San José.

The Park's fauna is well documented at the Information Centre.

Grass species endemic to the Canaries.

32

Left: the Teide red viper's bugloss.

Opposite page, above, the Teide daisy and blue viper's bugloss. Below, Izaña Astrophysical Observatory.

Laguna and from there on to the town of El Rosario, at which point the road enters the Monte de Esperanza pinewood. In what is a constant ascent, we arrive first at Izaña and then at Portillo de la Villa. From here, and without leaving the car, we can cross the volcanic depression as far as Boca de Tauce. Another recommended route starts from the tourist resort of Puerto de la Cruz in the north of Tenerife. We first head for La Orotava and from there we journey on through pines to Portillo de la Villa, right up amidst the mountain peaks. Yet another possible itinerary approaches the Park from the south, starting out from the tourist region encompassing Las Américas, Los Cristianos, El Médano and Reina Sofía Airport. This route climbs up to

Hiking near the Park.

Opposite page, the Parador.

Below, the Hermitage of Las Nieves.

The north coast as seen from El Sauzal.
Opposite page, view of the old quarter of La Orotava.

Below, La Orotava as seen from the Humboldt lookout point.
Two-page spread overleaf, San Marcos Beach at Icod.

Opposite page, banana trees (above) and windmill (below) in La Orotava.

This page, Casa de los Balcones (above) and tower of the Church of La Concepción at La Orotava.

Vilaflor and then on to Boca de Tauce. These are the most frequently used routes to the Park, but there are many others - to find them, one need only consult a road map. Once in the Park, the visitor must follow the instructions displayed by the authorities. It is advisable to go first to to the Visitors' Centre, where one is supplied with all kinds of information, especially if one wishes to use the various paths that lead around the Park. At the disposal of visitors arriving at the Park is a guide service, shelters, a picnic area, together with a Parador Nacional or state-run hotel open all year round and a cable-car lift that goes right up to the peak of El Teide, from where one can enjoy views of the other islands of the archipelago.

Puerto de la Cruz by night.

Lago Martiánez at Puerto de la Cruz. ▶

◄ Garachico.

San Miguel Castle at Garachico.

48

Los Realejos.   Right, Dragon tree of Icod de los Vinos.   Below, Buenavista del Norte.